# The Discovery Zone

*How to Successfully Navigate the
Changes and Transitions in Your Life*

**by Jerry M. Williams, Ph. D.**

**Vision Books**
Indianapolis, Indiana

Unless otherwise specified, all Scripture text
is taken from *The Holy Bible: New King
James Version*
©1988 Thomas Nelson, Inc.


**Copyright ©2001 by Jerry M. Williams**


**Published by Vision Books**
A division of Vision Communications / NCC Inc.
4625 North Keystone Avenue
Indianapolis, Indiana USA 46205
Printed in the United States of America
ISBN 1931425027

## DEDICATION

*To Joyce, and our children, Jason, Jerrae,
Jenelle, Jereel and Jeremiah.*

# Table of Contents

# Foreword

*"To live is to change, and to be perfect is to have changed often."* These words of John Henry Newman ring just as true today, if not more so, than they did in the nineteenth century. Change is inevitable, mandatory and unavoidable. The *only* issue before us is whether we will embrace change as the *evidence* that He who maketh all things new is up to something absolutely awesome in our lives. To resist is to fight against the one who says, "I am come that you might have life and have abundance."

"And after John had been taken into custody, Jesus came into Galilee, preaching the gospel of God, and saying, 'The time is fulfilled, and the kingdom of God is at hand; repent (*change* your mind) and believe in the gospel.'" (Mark 1:14,15) Jesus' proclamation of the gospel of God was the official announcement of the end of the old era and the beginning of the new. Luke confirms this when he says, "The law and the prophets were proclaimed *until* John; since then the gospel of the kingdom of God is preached, and everyone is forcing his way into it." In other words, radical change, chaos and general upheaval are the necessary precursors of signs, wonders and miracles.

Didn't John say, "I *must* decrease, but He *must* increase"? What do you care if the old order of guilt, shame, fear, pain, lack and failure leave your world with a bang or a whimper? In other words, the author of "The Discovery Zone" is saying when you're in the zone don't be distracted or intimidated by chaos. Keep your wits about you, being ever mindful, with joy, that "He who began a good work in you will perfect it." Yes, you will have experiences in the discovery zone that seem to shake you to the core, but remember:

1.    God is the shaker! Never lose sight of the fact that when it's all said and done, the shaking will leave you with the kingdom that cannot be shaken;

2.    Do not be threatened by the process of self-discovery. You're only losing what you cannot keep in order to gain what you cannot lose. It's only the Lord, with zeal for His temple, which you are, driving out the thieves and robbers. Afterward, Matthew declares that, "The blind and the lame came to Him in the temple, and He healed them." If you believe, you will see the glory of the Lord, "For the Egyptians (oppressors) whom you have seen today, you will never see them again forever."

Jerry and I have enjoyed sweet fellowship for many years, but it was especially in the discovery zone that I *discovered*, "There is a friend who sticks closer than a brother." Because he is one who continues to work out his revelatory insights in the zone with joy unspeakable and full of glory, I heartily commend him to all of you who are ready to embrace the adventure of adversity with joy and gratitude.

~ Paul L. Garlington

*Director of Heartsight Lifestyle Training Center,*
*Rochester, New York*

# Acknowledgements

I want to express my gratitude to my daughter, Jenelle Williams and two former Administrative Assistants, Katrina Sumner and Cynthia Glover, for the contributions they made in typing portions of the manuscript to make this book possible.

Thank you to my wife and children, who encouraged me and tolerated my sacrifice of time and energy to complete this book.

A special thanks to my long-time mentor and spiritual father, Paul L. Garlington, who has taught me so many deep truths about, God, His Word, life and the ministry.

I will always be deeply appreciative of Pastor Walter and Hattie Smith of Evangelist Crusaders Church, in Minneapolis, Minnesota for providing me a strong foundation in the Gospel ministry.

And, certainly I want to acknowledge all the wonderful people that I have pastored in congregations in Toledo, Ohio; Minneapolis, Minnesota; and Raleigh, North Carolina. Thank you for receiving my ministry. You have been an indispensable part of my change and transition process.

# Introduction

*The interval between the decay of the old and the formation and the establishment of the new, constitutes a period of transition which must always necessarily be one of uncertainty, confusion, error, and wild and fierce fanaticism.*

~John C. Calhoun, American senator

Welcome to the Discovery Zone. It has been often said that, to live is to grow and to grow is to change. Everyone experiences change. In fact, one's life could be characterized, in some sense, as a process of continuous change, i.e., circumstance after circumstance, event after event, occurrence after occurrence, situation after situation, etc. The objective of this writing is to assist the reader with understanding the change and transition process, and the opportunities it affords. Change doesn't occur in a vacuum. Change is change only because it ends something old and begins something new. Before you can experience a change in your life, you have to experience an end to what used to be.

Before you can become a new person, you must let go of the identity of the old person. You can't learn a new way of living, until you let go or unlearn the old way. A new beginning is predicated on an ending. The problem for most people is that, they don't like endings; therefore, they resist change or otherwise fail to make a transition from that which ended to a new beginning. Change and endings go hand in hand because change causes transition, and transition starts with an ending.

The Discovery Zone is the transition between endings and new beginnings. In this book, I will analogize one's personal change and transition process to Israel's experience when God ended their bondage of slavery in Egypt, their release from Pharoah's domination, their difficulty in starting a needed transition, their wilderness wondering, and their new beginning in the Promised Land. It will be easy to see and understand that the same change and transition principles that apply to the nation Israel are also applicable to individuals.

To help the reader to be sufficiently armed to deal with change, I will identify the phases of change and transition, with a view of Israel's experience and my personal reaction to some change events in my life. I will explore the way of the wilderness and set forth the necessity for wilderness preparation and, hopefully, provide an understanding of this highly emotional transition. I will deal with the nature of change and its implications; the challenges of transition—discovering things about God, yourself and others; coming face-to-face with the thoughts of your mind and the feelings of your heart; embracing the opportunities notwithstanding uncertainties; and, not yielding to the temptation to abort the process by seeking short-cuts to ease the emotional discomfort and pain.

God's promise to Israel, given while they were slaves, of a land that flowed with milk and honey, in order to be fulfilled, required an ending, a transition, and a new beginning. A new beginning implied that slavery would end. And to get from Egypt to the Promised Land necessitated a transition. Transitions are wilderness explorations. The wilderness is a desert place; an uninhabited place; a place of desolation and loneliness. It speaks of test and trials; discipline and humiliation; a time of proving; and, purification and preparation. This wilderness exploration and transition is the Discovery Zone.

## CHAPTER ONE

# The Discovery Zone

---

*So God led the people around by way of the wilderness...* **Exodus 13:18**

The way of the wilderness is a picture of change and transition. Just as life consists of a series of choices and consequences, it is also true that one's life is a succession of changes and transitions. Anyone who has experienced a change in his life has undoubtedly also faced a transition. Perhaps you're dealing with a change in your life now, or maybe you have begun to navigate your way through a transition. Is there a difference between a change and a transition? Absolutely. "Change" and "transition" aren't words that should be used interchangeably, not if you're going to successfully manage change and the challenges of transition.

Since change is not the same as transition,

what is the difference? Change is always situational, for example, a new job, a new church or ministry, a new assignment or a new budget or policy. Transition, on the other hand, is the emotional process one goes through to come to terms with the new situation. Change is always external; transition is always internal. Every change in your life means something has ended and something else has begun. Change and transition are about you and your individual journey through the changing situation. All of us, regardless of our stage in life, is subject to change and transition. All of us have gone through changes. All of us have faced changes, challenges, tests and trials without being done in. It's not the changes that challenge us; it's the transitions. I call these transitions **"The Discovery Zone."**

There's a marked difference between change and transition, and we need to know what's happening to us in these processes. Although change is not the same as transition, change will always give birth to a transition. Change is situational. You may change churches, change friends, change your address, get engaged, get married, get divorced, change jobs, get promoted, or experience the change of having a new baby born into your family. Now that's a real change.

As the father of five children, this writer, knows firsthand that every newborn addition to the family brings dramatic change. I also know that the real challenges for my wife and I began after we brought our new babies home. It wasn't the changes that stretched us—it was the transitions. The transitions presented an emotional process we went through to come to terms with the new situation, i.e., thoughts, feelings, and concerns about having adequate resources to provide for a growing family, the emotional reaction that the older children would display toward the newly born, and our need to adjust ministry, career, and educational plans in order to be the God-ordained primary caregivers of this new child.

Change is external. Change has to do with things that happen on the outside of us. Transition has to do with the things we feel, the things we think as we go through the process of trying to come to terms with the changes and the new situations in our lives. Transition always has to do with the psychological and emotional processes we go through when we are faced with a change—the things we think, the things we feel, and the things we have not uttered to a single soul. These internal things we go through have to do with the transition, not the change.

Once a change occurs, there's nothing we can do about it, but there is a lot we can do about the transition that results from the change. The discovery zone has to do with the internal transition process, and every one of us goes through that. It's like the guy who's about to get married. He's told everybody at his bachelor party, "Yeah, just as soon as tomorrow comes and she says 'I do,' I'm going to straighten her out. Don't worry about a thing, because I'm the man." Let me tell you something. This young man is in for a rude awakening and a big transition. If you have been married long enough, and especially if you've been married as long as I have (twenty-five years at this writing), you know you can't change that woman!

For this young man, the wedding is an external change, but after the wedding, after the ceremony and particularly after the honeymoon, the transition sets in. Now, he's got these thoughts going around in his head: "I wonder if I did the right thing. I didn't know she was like that." This is all part of the transition process.

In the discovery zone, your attitudes and feelings toward God, yourself and others are exposed. The emotional reaction to change and transition reveal's how you really feel about God, yourself and others. Moreover, it reveals your "truth" so you can't lie to yourself any longer. You are forced to deal with your feelings and emotions because you can't go back and undo the change. If you try to undo the change, you abort the transition. If you abort the transition, you've also forfeited the new beginning. There is no such thing as something changing without something ending. Something has to end. Something has to begin. If it doesn't end, it won't begin.

It is interesting to note that the Chinese language presents an interesting way of thinking about change. The Chinese character for "crisis" (what most of us experience when we're going through a significant change) is a combination of two characters "danger" and "opportunity." With every change we experience in life, there will be a sense of loss or a sense of gain. There will be danger, or there will be opportunity. A change can potentially hurt us, or a change can make us stronger, if we recognize the opportunity it affords. For example, if you feel like a changed situation has given you lemons in life, you still have the power of choice. You can either suck bitter lemons, or you can make lemonade. I believe God wants us to make lemonade out of the lemons we experience in life. I don't believe it's God's will for us to go around with a grotesque–looking face, with a grimace and a frown from the sucking of lemons. It's time to make lemonade!

## CHAPTER TWO

# Phases of Change and Transition

There are three phases in the change and transition process and we need to understand these phases. In doing so, we can better understand ourselves and those with whom we are in relationship. The first phase in the transition process is called *ending*. In other words, something has to end. The question is: what ended? The only way I can change jobs is to end my previous job. The only way I could relocate from Minnesota to North Carolina was by ending my residence in Minnesota. So the first phase in the change and transition process is an ending. Often with endings we feel a sense of loss. We feel a sense of grief. We find ourselves grieving over things and struggling to let go of the old situation or thing that has come to an end.

Nonetheless, we must be willing to let go. Otherwise it doesn't end. Some have mistakenly thought that something ended in their life, but they were still living it out in their mind and in their soul. They were still emotional over that thing because they refused to let it go. If they didn't let it go, it didn't end. If you don't let a thing go, it won't end! Instead of transitioning to a new beginning, you'll be stuck in a place between nowhere and somewhere!

According to William Bridges, author of *Managing Transitions*, the second phase of the change and transition process is called **exploration.** To me, this is a wilderness period. As mentioned earlier, I call this transitional phase the discovery zone. The discovery zone is just a temporary state of being between the old and the new. Perhaps by now you're beginning to realize that you are there now. You're between the old and the new, but while you're between the old and the new, you'll have opportunities for discovery. You'll discover things about yourself, you'll discover things about others and you'll discover things about your situation, but you'll also have opportunity for creativity and chaos!

In the discovery zone you will also find opportunity for chaos. You will feel like all hell has broken loose. Something changes in your life, and it seems like the breaking of a dam and the waters gush out and begin to flood your life. When you're experiencing chaos in your life, you need to do something about it. The thing you need to do is become creative. You have the ability to create. The first revelation in the Word of God about Father God is that God is a creator.

In the beginning, God created! We're made in the image and likeness of God. Therefore, if our Heavenly Father is creative, that means I have creative potential. If I'm going through a transition, and I'm finding myself in the mind-set of chaos, I'm finding myself as I go through the midst of the discovery process. I'm more sad than I am happy, and it's up to me, it's my responsibility, to take my chaos and my sadness and create some happiness!

You can sit around and mope all you want. But when you go through your transition process, you have to take responsibility for it. This is why it takes some of us longer to get through it than others. You know some people experience a change. They go through a very quick transition, and now they're on to new beginnings. Others get fixated on the end of whatever situation has ended. They are eating it, sleeping it, and can't think about anything else. They're preoccupied with what happened. We must recognize that the ending is the past. We need a transition to get to our new beginning and our future.

The third phase of the change and transition process is called **new beginnings**. Now understand something about new beginnings. You cannot experience a new beginning if something hasn't ended, and you can't experience a new beginning without a transition between something that ends and something that begins.

There is always a transition period. New beginnings never look like an instantaneous **END/ BEGIN**—never. Something has to end; then a transition period occurs; then, new beginnings. For most, it can be like this. For others, it may take forty years.

To help illustrate my point, let me use a television program analogy. Perhaps you have a favorite television program. Did you noticed that, no matter how much you want to see your favorite program, no matter how much you want to see your story, even though you're sitting in front of the television, five to ten minutes before your story is supposed to come on, your program can't begin until the previous program ends. I don't care if you turn the television on an hour early; your program will not begin until the previous program ends. That's the way it is in life. Something has to change. You go from one change in programming to the next. One program ends and the next program begins. Isn't this just like life's changes and transitions? Often times, the transition between programs is the trip we make to the refrigerator during commercials. But when the anticipated program comes on, it's a new beginning. You become energized in your excitement, yet feel some degree of uncertainty because you're not sure what will happen on today's episode. Notwithstanding the awkward feeling of uncertainty, new beginnings always present new opportunities and a real sense of renewal and revitalization.

## CHAPTER THREE

# The Way of the Wilderness Is A Discovery Zone

---

*Then it came to pass, when Pharaoh had let the people go, that God did not lead them by way of the land of the Philistines, although that was near; for God said, "Lest perhaps the people change their minds when they see war, and return to Egypt." So God led the people around by way of the wilderness of the Red Sea. And the children of Israel went up in orderly ranks out of the land of Egypt. And Moses took the bones of Joseph with him, for he had placed the children of Israel under solemn oath, saying, "God will surely visit you, and you shall carry up my bones from here with you." So they took their journey from Succoth and camped in Etham at the edge of the wilderness. And the LORD went before them by day in a pillar of cloud to lead the way, and by night in a pillar of fire to give them light, so as to go by day and night. He did not take away the pillar of cloud by day or the pillar of fire by night from before the people.* **Exodus 13:17-22**

Israel took forty years to make what should have been an eleven-day transition. It wasn't because God was so slow in delivering his promises; it was because Israel, in many ways, were slow learners, spiritually. They had to repeat their lessons, and you're going to repeat your lessons too until you learn them. God won't bring you into your future without a transition. He won't bring you into your new beginning until you learn what you need to during your transition. For Israel, something had to end, then there was a period between that which ended and that which began. Exodus Chapter 13 shows that, for Israel coming out of Egypt, the "way of the wilderness" was indeed a discovery zone. The discovery zone was a place where Israel found themselves after a change. After slavery in Egypt ended, Israel gave birth to a transition. In the discovery zone, as Israel experienced, you discover the awesomeness of God. You discover your destiny in God. You discover things about yourself that you didn't know about yourself. In the discovery zone, not only do you discover God and yourself, but you discover who your friends are. You discover who your enemies are. You discover if you really have believed

God; you discover if you're going to keep His commandments or not; you discover what's in your mind; and, you discover your real feelings (Deuteronomy 8:2). It all takes place in the discovery zone.

In Exodus 13:3-5, Moses said to the people: *"Remember this day in which you went out of Egypt, out of the house of bondage; for by strength of hand the LORD brought you out of this place. No leavened bread shall be eaten. On this day you are going out, in the month Abib. And it shall be, when the LORD brings you into the land of the Canaanites and the Hittites and the Amorites and the Hivites and the Jebusites, which He swore to your fathers to give you, a land flowing with milk and honey, that you shall keep this service in this month."* Moses is speaking to the people after Pharaoh had decided to let them go, after Pharaoh had decided to release them from the bondage, the degradation and the destitution of slavery. Something had ended for them. Legally, slavery ended for them. They didn't have to go down to the brickyards, as it were, to make bricks without straw. They didn't have to report to their hard taskmasters' houses to work without receiving a fair wage, because slavery had ended. But remember with every ending there is a transition before we enter into a new beginning. Moses is telling them about the process. He says, *"Remember this day in which you went out of Egypt, out of the house of bondage; for by strength of hand the Lord brought you out of this place.* No leavened bread shall be eaten." Here, Moses says something has ended, but there's going to be a new beginning. But between the ending and the new beginning, there would be a wilderness, there would be a discovery zone, there would be a transition.

We've pointed out what ended and what would begin for Israel. Now let's talk about the new beginning to get from where they ended, that is, from slavery to the place God promised them, the land of Canaan, a land overflowing with milk and honey. Verse 17 says, *"And it came to pass, when Pharaoh had let the people go...."* God did not lead them by the way of the Philistines although that was near. God is not a God of shortcuts. God takes us the long way home. God has a destiny for every one of us. God has a vision for every one of us. God has goals and objectives for every one of us. Your life is not by chance. You don't make this thing up as you go along. Even before the foundations of the world, God saw you. He chose you for a certain destiny in Him. God doesn't take us by the shortest route. He takes us by His route. His route depends on us, it depends on where we are, and it depends on our mental and emotional makeup. Sometimes, God takes us by ways that get things out of us. Even though Israel came out of Egypt, they still had Egypt in them (Numbers 11:5). Many of us have come out of darkness and the bondage of the world we lived in, but is that world out of us? Are you still holding on? Is there a sense of loss? Is there a sense of grief? You can't hang around with the same crowd any more. You can't go to places you used to go and, because you can't do what you used to do, you say, "well being saved is no fun." Then you wonder why its taking so long to come into the fullness you dreamed about, that which you believed, that which God promised you. No! God doesn't take us the shortest route. I don't know about you, but when I'm ready to go home, I'm invariably looking for a shortcut. But God, doesn't give us shortcuts. It's necessary to go through the process. To be all you can be in God, you've got to go through the process.

Why didn't God lead Israel by way of the land of the Philistines although it was near? Because God said, *"Lest perhaps the people change their minds whey they see war and return to Egypt."* God knew that even though His people had been liberated, even though His people had been released from the bondage of slavery, they still had slave mentalities. They were just raw recruits, just inexperienced rookies. They weren't ready to fight the Philistines. Another thing that secular history tells us about the way of the Philistines, is that the Egyptian armies often patrolled that road very heavily. Why would God bring you out of a bad situation just to put you into a worse situation? God did not deliver you out of the vile conditions you lived in, out of the house of ill repute you used to hang around in, just to send you back there. God didn't lift you up just to let you down. He didn't bring you in just to let you go out. God brought you where you are because He ended something. Now you're in a transition so that you can enter into a new beginning, a new future.

God said Israel wasn't ready. When they see war, they will change their minds and think and say that it was better to be slaves, because, at least, I was a living slave. A lot of people don't mind having a pharaoh in their lives. A lot of us don't mind being in bondage. A lot of us don't mind being in chains, as long as we can get gold chains. You don't want a ball and chain around your ankles, even if it glitters with 14-carat gold. You want to be free in God, and being free in God means that you are going through a transition process. Transition isn't the most comfortable experience. It will make us, it will break us, it will cause us to be everything God wants us to be. We will stand up and not fall, and when we enter into the promise, when we enter into the land, we will stand and not fall in the land. We will enjoy the goodness of God in the land. We will bring glory to God, and all nations that see us will know we're a delightsome land, and they too will give glory to God!

Okay *God led the people around by the way of the wilderness of the Red Sea.* Have you ever felt like your life was going around in circles, like you've passed this way before? God was leading you, just as He led Israel. God led Israel to the promised land, but not by a direct route. Most people, when traveling, want to take the most direct route. Why? Because they want to get to their destination in a hurry. It isn't that way in God. God will lead us around and about, intentionally.

So *God led the people around by the way of the wilderness of the Red Sea and the children of Israel went up in orderly ranks out of the land of Egypt.* Some other translations of the Bible translate this verse as, *"the children of Israel went up harnessed, the children of Israel went up armed, the children of Israel went up equipped."* What were they armed with? What were they equipped with? How could they have been harnessed when they were just slaves? Exodus Chapter 15 answers this query. When Israel finally crossed over the Red Sea, they had the song of the Lord. They had the praise of God in their hearts. They rejoiced because they had a promise from God.

When you have a word from God, when you

have the joy of the Lord, when you have a song in your heart, you are armed—the same way Jehosaphat's army was armed when they went out to fight the Moabites, the Ammonites and the children of Mount Seir (2 Chronicles 20). They didn't have carnal weapons such as swords and spears and other battle armaments. All they had was praise unto God. As they began to sing and praise God and say that "God is good and His mercy endures forever," their enemy was confounded, and they slaughtered and destroyed themselves thus giving God's people a great victory. I don't care what you're faced with today. I don't care what's standing before you, how wide it is or how tall it is. If you'll begin to praise God, if you'll begin to stand on the promises of God, if you'll begin to put a song in your heart, the giants will begin to look like midgets and the mountains will appear as mole hills. God led Israel about. He led them through the wilderness. It was a discovery zone. You need to understand what happens in the discovery zone.

## CHAPTER FOUR

# Understanding Wilderness Preparation

Understand what the wilderness is. The wilderness is a desert place. It's a place where nothing grows. It's a place where you're giving and giving and nothing comes back. You've been giving your tithes and offerings, but it seems like nothing's coming back. I want you to know you're in a discovery zone. It's a place where you sow, but the seed doesn't grow. It's a desert place. It's a place where there isn't moisture in the ground. It's a place where the rivers don't flow. It's a place of dryness. It's a place of hardness. It's an uninhabited place. It makes you feel like you're the only one out there, like you're the only one going through. I want you to know that even though you feel like you're in an uninhabited place, even though you may feel that you're in a place by yourself, you are not unique in terms of the tests and the trials.

You face the same things that all of us go through. The same things I go through, you go through. All God's children go through a discovery zone ordeal. The desert is a place of desolation. It's also a place of loneliness. It's a place where you discover firsthand what it's really like to be lonely. You don't know whom to talk to, whom to call, and you wish you could just be around somebody, but you're going through this hard place, and you feel like you're going through it alone. This is the discovery zone.

Understand that this discovery zone speaks of tests and trials. It speaks of discipline and humiliation. God has us in a place where He is requiring us to do things on a consistent basis. God is requiring us to do things perhaps that we haven't done before. You must stay in the Word, you must stay before God, you must stay in communication and communion with Him. You must acknowledge that the discovery zone is a place where God disciplines us. It's a place of humiliation. It's a place where you're looking to God for things to happen, but they seem to be happening for everybody but you. You think, "I've been sowing, I've been praying, I've been trying to live right, I've been trying to treat others right, but it seems like nothing good is happening in my life." You see other people being blessed with new cars, new homes, new clothes, and you think, "Dear God, when is my ship coming in?" Because you're in a discovery zone, you feel humiliated. Your thoughts and feelings begin to run rampant. "Seems like everybody's being blessed but me. Everybody's moving out of the "hood" but me. Everybody's getting a new car but me. I'm still driving down the road in my "hooty" with "Maypop" tires." You may be asking yourself, what are "Maypop" tires? What brand is that? Well, they're not Firestone, they're not Michelin, they're not BF Goodrich—they're "Maypop". In other words, they may pop anytime! But that's part of the discovery zone. It's a feeling of humiliation that none of us welcomes with open arms.

You're being disciplined. You're being humiliated. The discovery zone is a place where you're being proved. Not that you're proving things to God, but you're proving things to yourself about God. You're proving to yourself whether you're going to keep His commandments. You're proving to yourself whether you're going to stand and trust Him. You're proving to yourself whether you're going to wait until your change comes. It's a place of purification, a place where God will empty out of us all of the stuff we brought out of Egypt. A lot of Christians, even though they've come out of Egypt, still have a lot of Egypt in them. God will lead you through the discovery zone so He can purify you. He will take the tastes, the affections and the desires of the world out of you. Until God does it, it won't be done and He'll do it in the wilderness. He'll do it in the discovery zone.

We get confused because we can't understand why we still have an appetite for the things of the world. It's not because you're not saved. It's not because you didn't believe on the record of God's son. Something really did end, but bless God, you're holding on to something. You feel like you've lost something. You feel like being saved isn't that much fun. You may say to yourself, "Look at all the fun I used to have. My God ... I know I'm not supposed to do that, but I want to do that." You have this sense of loss because you're not doing the things you used to do, and you even grieve sometimes when your sinner friends look and sound like they're having a good time. This is all part of an emotional internal process. We need to understand how to deal with these thoughts and feelings. It is imperative that you be honest with yourself. It is also helpful if you can find people to be around with whom you can safely disclose with in total honesty.

You may remember that, while Israel was trekking through the wilderness, some of the weak Israelites, torn between Egypt and the promised land, were lagging behind in the congregation, and the Amalakites came from behind attacking and killing some of them (Deuteronomy 25:17-19). A lot of us are like that. We're still holding on to the past. We still have trouble letting go. We're lagging behind. Yes, we love God. We want to go on with God, but we're lagging behind, like the weak Israel-ites. The Amalakites, your enemies, are going to come from behind and attack, and you'll be destroyed. That's what happens when you're in the discovery zone, struggling with letting your endings go.

Another important thing that happens in the discovery zone is that God will prepare you. That which occurs between endings and new beginnings is a time of preparation. God is preparing you for greatness. God is preparing you for a bright future. If you're going into a new beginning, you've got to be prepared. You can't enter into the promised land saying, "The people, the inhabitants of this land, are so big and strong and tall, I look like a grasshopper in their sight." Please notice what God had to do. God had to kill off an entire generation of unbelieving Israelites who came out of Egypt before He could take them into the promised land, because almost an entire generation was still holding on to Egypt. Remember what they said, to Moses? "Why did you bring us out here? "We ain't got nothing to eat but this manna. We ain't got nothing to eat but this quail."(Numbers 11:1-6). They yearned for the fish, the onions, the garlic, and the leeks they ate in Egypt, and they said they missed what they ate in Egypt. Isn't it ironic that fish, onions, garlic and leeks are all foods that give you bad breath? God was trying to freshen them up but they wanted to continue in the stench of a dark ending.

For Israel, the wilderness was a place for preparation. We too must prepare for transition. Transition, in and of itself, prepares us for new beginnings. Here's what I learned in my experience. Preparation is necessary, most definitely. Nothing can take the place of preparation. After serving in the Kingdom of God in full-time ministry for almost thirteen years, my senior pastorate ended. To provide financial support for my family, I found myself back in the corporate world—not preaching and teaching, but using my abilities and talents in business operations, marketing and human resources management consulting. During the seven years I spent in the business world, I felt like I was in a wilderness.

My only consolation during this period of time was that wildernesses don't last forever. Do you know the feeling when something ends and a transition begins, and you find yourself doing things you really don't want to do, and wish you didn't have to do. I found myself giving corporate America my time, my talents and my efforts but they wanted my soul. I found myself being almost an object that corporate America owned. As a senior executive, the magnitude of my responsibilities did not allow me to leave my work at the office. Oh no, I had to take it home with me or, if I didn't get enough things done while in the office, then I didn't go home until I did. In order to succeed, I allowed my work to become more important than anything else. But God called me to preach; God put a burning passion and desire in my heart to share the good news of the gospel. So here, I am trying to stay on top in corporate America during this transition, preaching on the weekends, preaching revival meetings on my vacation time, and knowing that I had to go back to that office where I did not want to be, notwithstanding my job title and the money. Nothing in the workplace satisfied me, not the good salary and bonuses, not the perks, not the dignity and honor associated with having a coveted position in a world-class consulting firm. Notwithstanding, I was in preparation. I used to wonder, "Lord, how long is this thing going to take? I'm called to preach; I'm not called to be a businessman." I was in a transition for a long time— a wilderness of seven years. I suppose, had I learned some of the later lessons earlier on, my transition wouldn't have taken so long.

As you might surmise, I had trouble letting

go. When I resigned my senior pastorate in 1991, my family and I moved to Atlanta. The first thing I did, once we settled into our new home, was talk about starting a new church. But there was no confirming witness in the Spirit. I still couldn't let it go. In fact, there was another church in Atlanta that my sister pastored, under my oversight. She had decided to move out of state with her ministry, and she was waiting for me, the pastor without a congregation, to take over the work so that she could be released from the assignment. I thought, "I'll just take that church over because they need a pastor." Not so fast! My wife said, "not so," and the Holy Spirit made it clear to me that this was neither the time nor the season.

These kinds of things happen in the wilderness. You come so close, and yet you're so far away. Israel was eleven days yet forty years, away from the Promised Land. When you're so close yet so far, you can see it, you can taste it, but you just can't seem to seize it to enjoy it. But this is the discovery zone. In the discovery zone you must get to a place where you can say, "God, not only am I committed to you, but I am committed to the process. Whatever you need to do, do it in me. However long it takes, Lord, just do it in me, because I want to be everything you want me to be when I come out of this process. I don't want to have to go back and repeat my lessons. I don't want to have to go back to Egypt." You don't want to go back to that which has ended; you want to go on to something bigger and better. You want to go on to the new beginning—a land that flows with milk and with honey!

## CHAPTER FIVE

# Understanding Wilderness Transitions

There are some things you need to understand about the wilderness transition. There are some steps involved in this process of preparation that will enable you to identify these occurrences in your life as they relate to the various steps.

The first thing you need to understand about the wilderness transition is simply this: **transition begins with the letting go of something.** Even though there is a change in life, even though something has ended, you're still there. You haven't been able to move on because of the inability to let go. Sometimes you need to let go of certain individuals and relationships. You know the relationships are not productive. You know the relationships are not healthy. You know nothing good will come from these relationships, but because you're going through a transition, you're afraid to be alone. You're afraid you won't have anybody there when the lights go out at night. You hold on to bad relationships when, the reality is, you will not have a successful transition until you let go. You have to let unproductive relationships go. Just let them go.

If you're in a dead end street job, let it go. Getting in bad health, getting all stressed out, complaining, talking under your breath against your boss, just let it go! Get out of there! It's destroying you. You don't want to die in the discovery zone like many of the Israelites did. You don't want to die in the wilderness. You want to come into the land; you want to come into what God has promised.

The second thing in understanding the wilderness transition is this: *You must understand what comes after letting go and be mentally prepared for it*. After letting go comes the discovery zone. Another way of saying this is, after letting go comes the desert place, comes the uninhabited place, comes desolation and loneliness. After you let it go, the discipline is going to come. The tests and the trials, the humiliation, the proving. The preparation is going to come after you let it go.

The third thing you need to understand is this: *the discovery zone is a state of limbo between the old and the new.* You're in a state of limbo between the old and the new, between the old sense of identity and the new sense of identity. The old is gone, but the new just doesn't feel that comfortable yet. It will take some getting use to.

There are many individuals who have been divorced, many who have been widowed. Instead of understanding that something has ended and a transition is being birthed, they hold on to the former spouse. They hold on to the former boyfriend or girlfriend even though that relationship has ended. I've gone to funerals where people wanted to jump into the grave, just fall into the grave because they couldn't let go. "Take me," they would cry out. Theses persons were experiencing enormous difficulty letting go. It was painful for them to think that a relationship was ending after having companionship for so many years. So they try to hold on.

While some try to hold on to that which has ended, others rush through the transition, rather than allowing God to lead them through. They rush through a transition to find somebody else, a companion or partner. They find somebody else prematurely, while they're still holding on to the one they couldn't let go. Because they couldn't let the old one go, because they're still emotionally tied to the other, there are deep problems in the new relationship. They are still in love with the other. Even though they're with the new person physically, their mind and soul are with the other. It is imperative that you take your time through the transition process, discover God and discover yourself. If you enter the new too quickly, it won't feel right and it won't fit right.

## CHAPTER SIX

# Unless Transition Occurs, Change Will Not Work

*Every commandment which I command you today you must be careful to observe, that you may live and multiply, and go in and possess the land of which the LORD swore to your fathers. And you shall remember that the LORD your God led you all the way these forty years in the wilderness, to humble you and test you, to know what was in your heart, whether you would keep His commandments or not. So He humbled you, allowed you to hunger, and fed you with manna which you did not know nor did your fathers know, that He might make you know that man shall not live by bread alone; but man lives by every word that proceeds from the mouth of the LORD.* **Deuteronomy 8:1-3**

God said to Israel, after they crossed over into the Promised Land, after it had taken them forty years to make an eleven-day journey, "I am the One who led you about these forty years." Say what! Excuse me, Lord. Did I hear you say, "You led me all this way?" God is certainly behind what's happening to you in life (Romans 8:28). The Lord will orchestrate endings and transitions and keep you in a necessary transition as long as it takes for change to work in your life. Without transition and change, new beginnings are aborted.

Metaphorically, life is nothing more than a major theatrical production, and all of us are actors. The script has already been written, so we may as well cooperate with the director and get on with the show. I don't care how long you pray and fast, what sacrifices you make and what penance you do, if what you want from God isn't in the script, it won't be yours apart from shipwreck.

In the discovery zone we learn to live by listening. We listen to Gods voice, hear Him and have the opportunity to obey his commandments. If you can't hear God before a transition occurs in your life, you'll find yourself stuck in the wilderness, where you will learn to hear God and welcome his voice. Unlike the first generation, this was the lesson the second generation of Israel learned, by allowing God's transition to occur and change to take place in their hearts and minds.

Deuteronomy Chapter 8 outlines the principle that, when transition occurs, change will work; when change works, a new beginning follows. Let's walk through the first three verses. Verse one: *"Every commandment which I command you today you must be careful to observe, that you may live and multiply, ..."* God wants you to live and multiply? He wants you to have not only a good life, but a life full of abundance. He wants you to go in make your transition, and possess the land, that is, the promised blessings of a new beginning. He didn't say, just sing about it, just confess it. He said, GO IN AND POSSESS IT!

There are some things God wants us to possess before we confess. If all you're going to do is confess it, you may never possess it. Transition and change must be walked out, not just talked out. *...and go in and possess the land of which the Lord swore to your fathers."* These are words that God spoke to the first generation of Israelites, to whom the promise was initially made. With the exception of Joshua and Caleb, this first generation, who had experienced an end to slavery, failed to make a successful transition in the wilderness and, in so doing, had aborted God's promise of a new beginning in the land of Canaan.

Verse two: God continues to speak to the second generation. *"And you shall remember that the Lord your God led you all the way these forty years in the wilderness, ..."* Who led them through the wilderness? Who led them through a discovery zone?" God did! Well, why did God take so long during this transition? It was only in eleven-day journey. God took so long because Israel needed a long time to be taken. Listen to God's explanation of why this transition took forty years rather eleven days: " *...to humble you and test you, to know what was in your heart, whether you would keep [God's] commandments or not.*" Remember, the discovery zone is a place of humiliation; it's a place of tests and trials. It is also a place where you learn and know what's in your heart. It's a place of discovering God and discovering yourself and who you really are in God. Here, in this place, you move from belief to knowledge. You will know firsthand if you'll keep God's commandments or not. A lot of people have said, "Lord, if you bless me, I will go all the way." "Lord, if you just change my situation or circumstances, I will serve you, if you just open the door." Remember, in Exodus, 13:19 Moses took the bones of Joseph because Joseph had made the children of Israel swear by solemn oath that, after his death, they would not leave his bones in Egypt. Joseph wanted his bones carried back and buried in Canaan the country of his nativity. Moses remembered the promise and, when they began the transition out of Egypt, they took the bones of Joseph with them.

I believe God is saying to His people today. "There are vows you've made after something ended or to get something to end. In your transition to a new beginning, you are to remember the promise and keep your vows." You're to remember the promises you made, regardless of the challenges and hardships of transition. In the same way the children of Israel would not find rest until the bones of Joseph found rest, you will not find rest until that promise and that vow you made to God finds rest. You can't just leave it hanging out in the air. You've got to bring it to a place of rest and fulfillment.

God says in Verse 3: *"So he humbled you, allowed you to hunger, and fed you with manna which you did not know nor did your fathers know, that He might make you know that man shall not live by bread alone; but man lives by every word that proceeds from the mouth of the Lord."* Please notice that God did not allow them to starve, but he did allow them to get hungry in the wilderness, in the discovery zone. During a transition, God will allow our needs to intensify so that we will look to Him, hear Him and learn the necessary lessons of preparation. Regardless how serious the need in our life, God is faithful during the process to supply us what we need, but not necessarily what we want. He supplied Israel's need for food with manna, which they did not know, nor did their fathers know. In doing so, He wanted them to learn a lesson: that man shall not live by bread alone, but man lives by every word that proceeds from the mouth of God. Man lives by listening to God. Man is able to make a successful transition from something that ended to a new beginning by listening to and obeying the voice of the Lord.

When you are in the discovery zone, God will humble you through adverse and unfavorable circumstances but He will not forsake you. There may be days when you are hungry, but He won't let you starve. Even when you're between jobs and there's no money for new clothes and shoes, just as He did for Israel, He'll do for you. Your old clothes and shoes won't wear out. You may not have the latest style, you may not have what everybody else seems to have, but God says, "That's alright. I'll preserve you in the discovery zone. I'm right there with you, I won't allow you to be forsaken."

You have to go through the discovery zone, you have to go through your wilderness, and you have to go through a transition. Why? If a transition doesn't occur, change won't work. In other words, without a transition, without a discovery zone, there is no promised land. There is no milk and honey. There is no promise of life in abundance. There is no new beginning.

Is there a way to avoid or abandon this whole

idea about the wilderness, the discovery zone, and a transition process? Sorry. You can't abandon this mission like a scheduled space launch. God wants you to go to the moon, and the mission cannot be aborted. Why? If you abort the mission, you jeopardize the change. If you try to find a way not to go through the discovery zone, then you've also found a way not to receive the change, the new beginning. If you want the new beginning, you must go through the way of the wilderness. If you escape prematurely, somehow, from the discovery zone, you compromise the change and lose out on a great opportunity.

This is a light affliction that every one of us goes through. If you have marital problems, girlfriend/boyfriend problems, problems on the job, problems in your community, problems in life, problems in your mind, problems in your soul, problems in your body, those are all light afflictions, and they don't compare to the glory you will receive if you stay on course.

You don't want to abort the discovery zone. Resist the temptation to escape it prematurely. If you do, you'll lose out on a great opportunity in God. I believe God is raising up His people for greatness. If you want to be great in God, there's a great price to pay, and there's no price you will ever pay that God doesn't give you what it takes to pay it in full. This is why God's presence was with Israel in the form of a pillar of cloud by day and a pillar of fire by night. Even though they were going through a transition, they were still God's chosen people, but with a slave mentality. God had ended slavery, and this discovery zone transition in the wilderness was God's way of taking the slave mentality out of them and putting the mentality of a priest and a king and a conqueror in them. God was with them in the wilderness. Israel had only to look up and follow the cloud.

God's presence is always with you, even when the rough conditions of your discovery zone seem unbearable. Even though it seems that God has abandoned you in a desert place, you should stay the course and refuse to abort the process. Just remember to look to the pillar of cloud and refuse to move until the cloud lifts and moves. If the cloud doesn't move, then stay still and see the salvation of the Lord. God's pillar of cloud by day is there to protect you from the heat and the fierce elements, not allowing the test and trials to destroy you. Yes, you can stand; you don't have to fall. You can stand in the midst of the fiery furnace, because God is a pillar of cloud by day. He's a pillar of fire by night. When darkness sets in and you can't see your way, God will be your light in the night. Just follow God.

God's presence, as a cloud and a fire, accompanying Israel in the wilderness, was a theophanic presence. God became a physical presence and manifestation of Himself. God showed up as the Shekinah glory right there in the desert. The people of God didn't have the best clothes and shoe or the best training. They were just raw rookies and recruits, but they were on their way to destiny. They were on their way to a land that flowed with milk and honey. They were on their way to a new beginning.

As the Lord was a theophanic presence in the furnace of fire with Shadrach, Meshach and Abednego (Daniel 3:25), the Spirit of the Lord showed up and guided the children of Israel through their discovery zone. God will show up in your process, if you're determined to go through your discovery zone. If you refuse to abandon the transition, refuse to compromise in any way, then great opportunity of a new beginning will be yours.

In the discovery zone you discovered the real you, and you feel good about your transformed self. For example, you can take a bum out of the gutter, and you can put him in a three-piece pin-stripe suit. You can give him a hair cut and a shave, you can manicure his nails and take him to the highest office tower and place him in an office suite and say, "Okay, Mr. Bum, you're now a businessman." If that bum hasn't ended being a bum emotionally and psychologically, if he's still holding on to his bumhood, to the fears and insecurities of the past, if he's still holding on to the sense of loss of not hanging out with his bummy friends, he will not succeed as a businessman. He will fall flat on his face, because he failed to make the transition. He failed to go through the discovery zone. You can take a person from rags to riches, you can take somebody out of abject poverty, you can let someone hit the lottery and win millions of dollars. After a while the millions will be gone and they'll be back in want. Why? Because even though they hit the lottery and became rich, they still had a poverty mentality in them. You can take somebody out of the ghetto, but you can't always take the ghetto out of him or her. When you can get the ghetto out of them, then they will be free. You have to make the transition or you're still the same old person you used to be. The children of Israel were no longer slaves; yet, God had to get the slave mentality out of them before they could experience a new beginning.

## CHAPTER SEVEN

# Walking Through the Discovery Zone

_____

Can you think of a situation in your personal life, your work life, your church or ministry in which you were required to undergo a significant change? This situation should be one which was initially something very challenging or dramatic for you, and perhaps those around you, but eventually it worked out successfully. Whether the change event was marriage or divorce, starting, losing or changing a job or relocating to a new state, somehow, with the help of the Lord, you worked through that individual change. The Psalmist declared that,

_The steps of a good man are ordered by the LORD, And He delights in his way. Though he fall, he shall not be utterly cast down; For the LORD upholds him with His hand._ **Psalm 37:23,24**

I would paraphrase verse 23 above as, "the

goings of a strong, change-hardy man are established and prepared by the Lord, who takes pleasure in his journey in the course of life." You see, a transition is our personal response to change. While change occurs as an event or series of events, a transition occurs within you—emotionally-psychologically—in distinct, yet subtle, phases.

### Working Through Change One Step At A Time

Changes are external by definition and are mostly beyond your control. On the other hand, a transition is internal and, therefore, subject to our understanding that the Lord is in control of the course of our lives. The Lord will order your steps in the discovery zone, through each phase-ending, wilderness, and new beginning.

It is natural to feel the desire to manage our lives during change and try to influence the outcomes of change as much as possible. But, if we are to satisfy our need to make change meaningful to us on our journey, we must understand that it is not only an emotional-psychological transition process, but, more importantly, that it is the Lord who is ordering our steps in our discovery zone. We can then adjust our lives by letting go, repenting, and making new choices, to better cope with the dangers and seize the opportunities in the discovery zone.

Whether you perceive the change as positive or negative, you will always experience a transition. Remember, it isn't the changes that do us in, it's the transitions. Transition is the emotional-psychological process we go through, punctuated by a lot of spiritual turmoil, in an attempt to come to terms with the new situation.

### Step One - Ending

When something ends in our life, we may experience a loss of identity, control, meaning, sense of belonging, a loss of turf, lost relationships, an absence of structure. We react to this sense of loss with feelings of guilt, fear, resentment, anger, shock and denial. These feelings will persist to the extent that we have difficulty letting go of what has ended, has been changed, or has been lost. It may be tempting to rush forward ahead of the Lord, so it is imperative that you pay attention to your emotional and spiritual needs during this phase. Losses can, at first, seem more evident than gains but remember that there will be a new beginning!

### Step Two - Wilderness Exploration

After the external change occurs, the internal transition process is set in motion. While God has brought us to a place on our journey where we can explore new opportunities, emotionally we find ourselves resistant to change, and we struggle with the unknown. In the wilderness, much like Israel did, we fluctuate between feelings of chaos and creativity, evidenced by the reactions of fear, anger, frustration, confusion, stress, approach-avoidance, skepticism, acceptance, impatience, and hope. Our challenge at this juncture is to manage our fears in order to explore the future possibilities. Yes, dangers will tend to stand out in this phase, but you must consciously focus on the opportunities the Lord presents and get ready for your new beginning by identifying the direction in which you believe God is leading you.

### Step Three - New Beginnings

You may not always recognize when the new beginning begins. In fact, new beginnings can feel a little shaky but exciting at the same time. Nonetheless, to transition into a new beginning you must make a commitment to follow wherever the Lord is leading. You must overcome the feelings of anxiety and fear and act on what you believe with energy and enthusiasm to achieve your new beginning. ***Though he fall, he shall not be utterly cast down; For the LORD upholds him with His hand. (Psalm 37:24).***

### Our Steps Are Ordered By the Lord

The Lord, through the discovery zone, orders our steps, and He delights in our way. Begin with letting go of something. Even though it may feel like the gates of Hell are prevailing against our dreams and vision, the Lord is there! When you're in that low place, between the former somewhere and the next somewhere, between the old sense of identity and the new, when the old is gone and the new doesn't feel comfortable yet, the Lord is ordering your steps. Unless the Lord orders your steps through the discovery zone, change will not work!

Everything that happens to you in each phase and at each step in your discovery zone is what God uses to help you redefine where you have come from in order that you may learn where to go. The discovery zone is the place where you learn how to work through chaos and reshape it by standing on the promises of your future (new beginnings). This process will, undoubtedly, press on you to accomplish more in your life than you thought possible (Jeremiah 29:11). Because the discovery zone transition processes are emotional, psychological and spiritual, the journey from ending to new beginnings will lead you to experience radical transformation (Romans 12:2).

## CHAPTER EIGHT

# The Longest Distance Between Two Points is a Shortcut

_____

*Then it came to pass, when Pharaoh had let the people go, that God did not lead them by way of the land of the Philistines, although that was near; for God said, "Lest perhaps the people change their minds when they see war, and return to Egypt." So God led the people around by way of the wilderness of the Red Sea. And the children of Israel went up in orderly ranks out of the land of Egypt ... So they took their journey from Succoth and camped in Etham at the edge of the wilderness.* **Exodus 13:17-18, 20**

Have you ever tried to take a shortcut to your destination? I'll never forget some of the bad experiences I've had trying to take short-cuts. When I first moved to North Carolina, I lived in a very small town. One day, I was in a hurry while driving in my automobile. I figured that most small towns are pretty much the same. If you've been through one you've been through all. I wanted to take a shortcut to get to my destination, so I took a left turn and ended up facing a dead end. I decided to take another left turn to try to find my way out and ended up sitting in front of railroad tracks impatiently watching a train go by. What I thought was a shortcut was really the longest distance between two points. Had I stayed on the prescribed route, the known way, I would have reached my destination much sooner.

I believe very strongly that when we are going through a wilderness experience, in other words, when our lives are in a discovery zone transition, it's important to stay the course. If you're tempted to take a shortcut, you may find that the longest distance between two points, i.e., ending and new beginnings, is a shortcut.

Remember, unless transition occurs, change will not work. It just won't work. Many have gone from change to change, but nothing is working out. Often people say, "Well I'm going through a lot of changes." Isn't it amazing how people go through changes and remain the same. The reason everything around us changes, yet we remain the same is that we have not gone through a transition process. We have looked for a shortcut. We have tried to escape. Unless you go through a transition process, you can have one change after another change and everything will still be the same. Unless transition occurs, change will not work, and you won't experience your new beginning.

I believe God wants to give everyone of us a new beginning. That which is old, that which is stale, that which is tasteless, God wants to give us something fresh—a new beginning. There's an old French saying, *"The more things change, the more they stay the same"* (Alphonse Karr, 1849). What was Karr saying? There can be any number of changes in your life, and all of us go through changes. The things you're going through are not unique to you. Have you considered that there are a lot of people having a worse time than you can even imagine? There can be a number of changes in your life, but unless there are transitions, nothing will have changed when the dust clears. You can be in the midst of a dust storm and say, "I'm going through one change after another, but when the dust settles, everything's the same." Why? It really isn't the changes that do us in. It really isn't the changes that really make us. The thing that makes us and the thing that really challenges us is the transition. These transitions are a discovery zone.

The discovery zone is the way of the wilderness. When God led the children of Israel out of Egypt, He did not lead them through the land of the Philistines, even though that was near, but He led them round about the way of the wilderness by the Red Sea. In other words, God didn't take them on an eleven-day journey, He took them on a journey of forty years before Israel could enjoy a new beginning. In the wilderness of life, the longest distance between two points is a shortcut.

### The Way of the Wilderness Starts With An Ending And Finishes With A New Beginning

The way of the wilderness always starts with an ending and finishes with a new beginning. Something has to end, but the discovery zone process doesn't end until something new begins.

When Pharaoh let the children of Israel go, that was an ending—the end of legal slavery in Egypt; however, the emotional bondage wasn't finished yet. The process was only starting. The way of the wilderness wasn't finished until Israel came into Canaan, where every place the soles of their feet trodded upon, they began to feel the joy of it. They began to enjoy, as it were, the milk and the honey. In other words, they began to walk into a new beginning. So the wilderness began when slavery ended, and it didn't end until Canaan land began.

Between Egypt (ending) and Canaan land

(new beginning) there were a whole lot of changes going on among the Israelites, changes such as freedom, no brickyards to work in, no tough taskmasters to answer to and obey, no fleshpots to eat from, no Egyptian culture.

When we talk about change, we often focus on outcomes the change produces. The Apostle Paul understood change and outcomes as evidenced in what he wrote to the Corinthian Christians. "Therefore, *if anyone is in Christ, he is a new creation; old things have passed away; behold, all things have become new* (2 Corinthians 5:17)." Being made a new creature is an outcome. If you are in Christ, you've been changed. The change is that God doesn't look at you as an old creature. He looks at you as a new creature. The reason some others still look at you as an old creature and the reason you may look at yourself as an old creature— is because, even though there's been a change, there hasn't been a transition. Being a new creature is an outcome, but you've still got to make that transition.

Every change in our lives produces outcomes. Outcomes are consequences that result from the change. For example, I lived in Alamance County, but when I changed my residence to Wake County, that was an outcome that produced consequences. When I left Alamance County to relocate to Wake County,

I had to travel fifty-seven miles across several counties in North Carolina. I had to pass through Alamance County, Orange County and Durham County before I got to Wake County. When I got to Wake County, I had to find my way around and find out where everything was located because I wasn't familiar with the territory. Now that was a change, and I was focused on the consequential outcomes, i.e., the feelings of unfamiliarity, the anxieties of getting lost from time to time, finding a new dry cleaner and places to shop in Wake County.

When you start a new job, you begin to focus on what outcomes that new responsibility will produce. It may be different working hours, it may be more pay, and it may be a longer commute. When you have a new baby born into the family, what are some the outcomes produced? It may mean sleepless nights, or being less spontaneous than you would like to be. You just can't run out at the drop of a hat or say to your spouse, "Let's go dancing. Let's go to the movies." You have a baby now. You may not have as much money to spend on yourself as you did before the baby was born, let alone money to pay baby-sitters. These are all outcomes produced by the change of having a newborn in your family.

Attending a new church? There are also outcomes produced with a new church. When you join another church, it won't be like the church you left. The biggest outcome and change produced is that you will have a new pastor and pastor's wife. I used to tell folks who came to the first church I pastored in Ohio that if they wanted me to be like their former pastor, then they should go back and be with their former pastor. Even when it came to my wife, some new members would say, "Well, Sister Joyce (my wife) doesn't act like a pastor's wife." Without hesitation I would retort, "She is my wife, and I wasn't married to your former pastor's wife. If you want my wife to be like your former pastor's wife, then you need to go back there." When you deal with a change, you focus on the outcomes produced, but it is different with a transition.

When change occurs in our lives, we often think the change is everything that's happened. No it isn't! Remember, change is situational. The change is external, but the most important thing is to deal with the transition. The transition has to do with the emotional, psychological, and spiritual process. It has to do with the things you're thinking, the things you're feeling, the things you're going through internally, the things that are going to move you, stop you, or stall you from reaching your desired new beginning.

You must deal with your feelings after every

ending in your life.   When slavery ended for
Israel, the starting point for their wilderness
transition wasn't the outcome. The outcome
that this change produced would have been
Canaan land—a land flowing with God-prom-
ised prosperity. When you experience a wilderness transition, the starting point is never the
outcome, but the ending, of something. You
must ask yourself, "What has ended?" If nothing has ended, then there was no change.
When something ends, then you'll have to
make a decision to leave the old situation. If
you can't leave the old situation, if you can't let
go, then you can't go through a transition
process. If you can't go through a transition
process, you can't enter the promised land.
You can't enter into a new beginning. You're
just stuck!

I often talk to people who are stuck. They're
stuck on something that happened many years
ago, something that ended for them ten years
ago, but what have they done for the last ten
years? They have not gone through a transition— they're stuck.

Even though you've been set free, you don't
want to get stuck in Egypt! There are a lot of
people who've been set free, by the power of
God, by the authority of the Word of God. Many
people have responded to the good news of
Jesus Christ, believed in the record of God's

son, but they're still stuck at the edge of the wilderness like Israel was.

*So they took their journey from Succoth and camped in Etham at the edge of the wilderness* (Exodus 13:20). Israel was still in Egypt after God ended their bondage of slavery. They came to Etham and stood there; they camped at the edge of the wilderness. When God sets you free, you don't want to camp at the edge of the wilderness. You want to cross over to the other side. You don't just stay there and thank God you're saved. No! God wants you to cross over your Red Sea. He wants you to cross over into the wilderness so you can head out to Canaan land.

Transitions are different than the actual change event. The way of the wilderness always starts with an ending. But the starting point for a wilderness transition is **not** the outcome but the ending that you will have to make in order to leave the old situation behind. Transition begins with something that ends. You've got to let it go if you're going to enter into the desired blessings or promise of the new beginning.

Every transition ushers in new and different feelings. Sometimes when you're trying to deal with the new feelings, you're still struggling with the old feelings. You've got to deal with the much-needed new mind-set as you

struggle with the old mind-set. You must have
the mind of Christ: *"Let this mind be in you
which was also in Christ Jesus,"* (Philippians
2:5). Colossians 1:13 says, "He has delivered
us from the power of darkness and conveyed
us into the kingdom of the Son of His love," "He
has delivered us ..." That's an ending. If God
has delivered us, that means that something
has ended.

What did God deliver you from? Whatever
it was, if He delivered you from it, it ended. You
may still be struggling with it. It may still be in
your mind and in your soul. Perhaps you still
have a desire for it and have affections for it.
Perhaps you still want it. But the Word of God
says, if something ended, God has delivered
you. "Has delivered," grammatically, is past
tense. When something ends, Colossians 1:13
also says there has to be a transition process:
"He has delivered us from the power of darkness and **conveyed** us into the kingdom of the
Son of His love."

Can you see why people struggle with endings in their lives? People struggle, although
they're sincere. They struggle because they
don't understand that, when Egypt ends, something else must begin as a transition process to
where God wants us. When Pharaoh let the
children of Israel go, they were free people,
legally. But in their minds, they still had the

mentality of slaves. In their minds, they still had a dependent mentality and a hand-me-out mentality. They did have enough sense to go to their neighbors and borrow jewelry and ask for the wealth—silver and gold and the fine things of Egypt and they took that out with them.

Even though we have come out of Egypt, even though God has delivered us from darkness, many are still struggling with Egypt inside of them. Now that they've come out of Egypt, they must somehow get Egypt out them. You've got to get the old stuff that ended out of you.

When Pharaoh let Israel go, he let all the Israelites go. When God saves, he saves all who respond to His message. Everyone who responds to the Word with a heart of faith is saved. But sometimes they don't feel like they're saved. They don't think like they're saved. They don't act like they're saved, because they are still holding on to the things of Egypt. That's all they've known. All the Israelites knew was Egypt. Until they let go, the transition process could not start. Had they never let go, they would never have entered into the Promised Land. I believe God wants to give all of us a new beginning. Every one of us needs a new beginning. It's time to move on in your life.

You can address discovery zone issues on a

corporate-organizational level, as well as on an individual level. An organization can't move on to fulfill its mission until the people involved in that organization move on—transition from their personal endings to new beginnings. All the talk about a vision doesn't mean anything if there's an unwillingness to move on. You're just spitting in the wind until people involved in the organization get a vision for their own lives. In fact, how are you going to help the organization realize the corporate vision when you can't help yourself with your own vision?

The new beginning hinges on a situational change, but the duration of your wilderness transition depends on how long it takes you to let go of the old reality and identity you had before the change took place. The temptation around the length of time is where the enemy gets us in trouble. You may even question your own salvation in Jesus Christ because of your personal struggle and length of time it takes to let go of the old reality and the old identity of living as a sinner. Yes, you are saved by God's grace (Ephesians 2:8), but how long is it going to take you to rid yourself of that old sense of identity of living in a world of sin; that old identity of how much fun you had when you were there?

You've got to get rid of that old reality and that old identity you had before the change took place. Otherwise, you're just stuck at the edge of the wilderness, Pharaoh has let you go but, because you haven't crossed over, he's coming to get you. The Roman Christians who were facing a similar struggle were admonished by the Apostle Paul, *"And do not be conformed to this world, but be transformed by the renewing of your mind, that you may prove what is that good and acceptable and perfect will of God (Romans 12:2)."* In other words, the situational change in this verse would be the good, the acceptable, and the perfect will of God. Many Christians are still struggling with the "not so good, the unacceptable, and the imperfect will of God." Obviously, they haven't made the transformation yet. They haven't gone through a successful transition process. Remember that this process is something that occurs inside of you. You've got to come to grips with these things on the inside of you. You've got to bring the way you think and feel under control, bring them under subjection to the word of God, in line with the spirit of God (2 Corinthians 10:5).

During a wilderness experience, the process will be transforming. You must go through a metamorphosis. For example, it's not enough to say that Jesus has set you free. It's not enough to say you're saved and, when you die, you're going to Heaven. In the same way, it wasn't enough when Pharaoh let Israel go. Israel went out and camped at the edge of the wilderness. But they needed a transformation. They needed a metamorphosis. They needed to be transformed by the renewing of their minds. Only after that process, starting with an ending and finishing with a new beginning, could they prove what was the good, the acceptable and perfect will of God.

## CHAPTER NINE

# Shortcuts Are Tempting

---

*And when Pharaoh drew near, the children of Israel lifted their eyes, and behold, the Egyptians marched after them. So they were very afraid, and the children of Israel cried out to the LORD. Then they said to Moses, "Because there were no graves in Egypt, have you taken us away to die in the wilderness? Why have you so dealt with us, to bring us up out of Egypt? Is this not the word that we told you in Egypt, saying, 'Let us alone that we may serve the Egyptians?' For it would have been better for us to serve the Egyptians than that we should die in the wilderness." And Moses said to the people, "Do not be afraid. Stand still, and see the salvation of the LORD, which He will accomplish for you today. For the Egyptians whom you see today, you shall see again no more forever. The LORD will fight for you, and you shall hold your peace."* **Exodus 14:10-14**

Remember the children of Israel were camped at Etham, the edge of the wilderness. They had not crossed over the Red Sea yet. Although they had been set free, they were still at the edge of the wilderness. Even after Pharaoh decided to end Israel's enslavement and let them go, he further decided, in his fierce anger, to go after them in a hot pursuit. Have you ever had "Pharaoh" come after you? You must realize that after something ends in your life, the "Pharaohs" of your world will come after you, too. This is what makes shortcuts so tempting to us—the fear of "Pharaoh" and the painful past that it represents.

Shortcuts are tempting because the way of the wilderness is a very emotional transition. It is an emotional rollercoaster. There's a time when you feel the joy of your salvation and deliverance because Jesus has set you free. There are times when you are excited and you're full of energy. Then "Pharaoh" decides to come after you. "Pharaoh" begins to draw near. You begin to see that the enemy has not left you alone; the enemy hasn't given up on you.

One of the reasons why the enemy hasn't given up on you is because you haven't given up on the enemy. The enemy will come and will try to pull you back into the darkness of Egypt.

He'll try to pull you back into the degradation and the destitution of being a slave without power, without authority, without experiencing freedom in Christ. He'll try to pull you down in life...he'll come after you.

Look at Israel's emotional turmoil. *So they were very afraid, and the children of Israel cried out to the Lord* (v.10). *Then they said to Moses, Because there were no graves in Egypt, have you taken us away to die in the wilderness?* (v.11). Of course not! I want you to know that when you're going through a transition process, your wilderness experience is not a time to die, it's a time to prepare to live. As in Israel's case, God is preparing you for life—life in a new beginning not death. The enemy wants you to think that you are going to die in the wilderness. But God says that's where He's going to teach you how to live. He further says "I'm going to teach you that man shall not live by bread alone, but by every word that proceeds out of the mouth of God." Regardless of how intense the emotional storm, this is not a time of death; this is a time of life.

They said to Moses, *Why have you so dealt with us, to bring us up out of Egypt? Is this not the word that we told you in Egypt, saying, Let us alone ...?* (vvs.11-12). No! The Israelites never said such things to Moses. In fact, they were glad to drop those bricks and chains of slavery. They were overjoyed to leave Egypt. They never told Moses to leave them alone. What's happening here? You must remember that change and transition is an emotional rollercoaster. For example, have you ever found yourself talking to someone in the middle of an emotional storm resulting from a difficult transition in his or her life? Isn't it interesting that such persons hear things that weren't said, see things that never occurred, and sometimes manufacture outright lies? Please understand that such a person isn't necessarily a liar. It may simply mean that they're on an emotional rollercoaster. When one is riding this emotional turmoil, it isn't clear who you are and what is real. You may feel confusion and think that something is wrong with you. The typical reaction is to try to escape or find a shortcut, which often manifests in irresponsible behaviors because you're frightened in this no-man's land. We need to understand ourselves, and we need to understand one another when passing through this difficult zone. We can begin to foster such understanding by refusing to pin on others negative labels when they're only going through a transition.

There is a tendency to invent things in your mind when you're on an emotional rollercoaster. People will invent thoughts about their boss, co-workers, a family member, spouse, their church and its leadership, because they are going through a transition. The children of Israel said to Moses, *...For it would have been better for us to serve the Egyptians than that we should die in the wilderness* (v.12). Let me say it again. The wilderness experience is not an experience to bring us to death, rather, it is an experience to prepare us for a victorious life.

## The Problem With Shortcuts

Shortcuts are tempting because of the emotional aspects of a transition. The pain seems greater than the gain, and because the pain distracts you, you don't exercise your faith to hear what God is saying and to see what God is doing in the situation. For example, there are a lot of people who have had significant changes in their lives. Some have been faced with a mountain of debt and had, seemingly, no choice but to file for bankruptcy. There's no reproach in bankruptcy. Bankruptcy is not only a legal remedy, it's a very scriptural remedy based on the Year of Jubilee (Leviticus 25). If you're in a mountain of debt and file bankruptcy, something has ended. Your debts have come to an end, because your creditors have been legally ordered to discharge you from those debts. But, if you don't go through a transition process, if you don't deal with the associated feelings and emotions, then you are going to have the same charge-it-now-pay-for-it-later patterns that led you to a mountain of debt. Why? Because you didn't experience change. You were freed from your debts, but now you're back in debt because you didn't go through a transition process. You were merely looking for shortcut. But there are no short-cuts if you are to experience genuine change and transition.

The Lord does not lead us the most direct way; He leads us His way. He will always lead you on His route, not the most direct route. When you're tempted to take a shortcut as you are embarking on a wilderness transition, you undoubtedly are dealing with all the emotional highs and lows. Let me summarize three things that happened to Israel and can also happen to you, as seen in Exodus 14:10-14.

First, because transition can be so emo-tional, sometimes it isn't clear who you are and what's really real. Israel had just been set free. They knew that Moses and Aaron were doing everything they could to obtain their freedom. They knew about the plagues that God brought upon Egypt. They knew about the miracles. They knew about the interviews that Moses and Aaron had with Pharaoh saying, "God said let my people go." They also knew they were chosen of God. Now that God has effected their freedom, they were at the edge of the wilder-ness and had forgotten who they were. They lost sight of the promised new beginning. Their vision of freedom became cloudy. If you're not careful, when you're going through a wilderness transition and find yourself in the discovery zone, you'll lose sight of your vision too. You can lose sight of who you really are and whose you are. You won't know what's really real. You'll begin to think and say that being back in your "Egypt" situation was more real than the promise God has offered you. So, the first thing that can happen is that things become unclear and your vision becomes dim and cloudy.

Second, you'll feel confusion and begin to think that something is wrong with you. Confusion is a very unsettling and uncomfortable feeling. Look how confused the Israelites were. In Verse 12 they told Moses to leave them alone so they could continue in slavery. But they didn't tell Moses that. They were confused because Pharaoh's great army was in hot pursuit of them. For them, it was like every demon from hell was trying to chase them down. They became confused. They were experiencing a great deal of emotional pain and forgot who they were and where they were going.

Third, you'll feel fear. Fear sets in at a time when you need to be standing in faith. Moses said to the Israelites, *"...Do not be afraid. Stand still, and see the salvation of the Lord ...The Lord will fight for you ... "* (Exodus 14:13,14). If you have faith in God's promise of a new beginning and stand still, God will fight for you in your transition.

You don't need a shortcut when you're going through a wilderness transition. You most definitely need faith in God. When Pharaoh comes after you, don't seek a shortcut, seek God. God will never leave you or forsake you.

James 1:2-4 outlines the real problem with shortcuts:

*My brethren, count it all joy when you fall into various trials, knowing that the testing of your faith produces patience. But let patience have its perfect work, that you may be perfect and complete, lacking nothing.*

When Pharaoh came after Israel, it was Israel's faith that was on trial. Pharaoh didn't realize that he was going up against God himself. He didn't know that his arms were too short to box with God. He thought he was going to fight against a defenseless slave people. But he wasn't going to fight with people who were slaves, people who didn't understand warfare. Unbeknown to him he was going against God Himself. It's your faith on trial during the discovery zone transition process. The enemy wants to destroy faith—that which can totally deliver you and set you free—your faith in God.

The Apostle James said, count it all joy. You must have a feeling of joy on your journey. When you ride the emotional rollercoaster, feel the joy or get out of the car. You've got to learn to enjoy the ride. Remember, success is not your destination, it's the journey. If you really believe that, then you had better feel the joy!

Don't look back and don't look for a shortcut, but let patience have her perfect process in you. Let patience have her perfect work. If you do, you're going to be perfect, complete, entirely lacking nothing in God, wanting nothing. You'll be blessed beyond measure. Blessed rising up and blessed lying down. Blessed coming out of your ending and blessed going into your new beginning.

The shortcuts will always compromise and jeopardize the new beginning. A shortcut invites chaos and confusion. When you look for a shortcut, you'll find chaos and confusion. You had better stay on the right road, the straight and narrow. God will see you through.

The way of the wilderness teaches you, it renews you, and it develops you in preparation of the new beginning. If you won't let patience have her perfect work, then you'll be unrenewed, unprepared, and undeveloped. When you attempt to shortcut the process, God will take you back to square one every time, so you can learn the lessons of yesterday to be prepared to walk in the promises of tomorrow. You can either learn it now, or you can learn it later. The new beginning, whatever it is in God for you, will wait patiently for you. Although the new beginning is ready for you, you may not be ready for it. Because you think you are ready, are you going take a shortcut because change didn't come when you thought it should? God forbid. The change of a new beginning is waiting patiently for you. It already exists in God's economy. It was waiting for Israel and it is waiting for you too. Though it was ready for Israel, Israel wasn't ready for it. The new beginning will wait for you until you are perfect, entire, wanting nothing. You can learn this now or you can learn it later. You can pay the price now or you can pay it later, or you can just die in the wilderness like the first generation of Israelites who came out of Egypt, except Caleb and Joshua (Deuteronomy 1: 30-36).

## CHAPTER TEN
# Go Forward and Don't Look Back

---

And when Pharaoh drew near, the children of Israel lifted their eyes, and behold, the Egyptians marched after them. So they were very afraid, and the children of Israel cried out to the LORD. Then they said to Moses, "Because there were no graves in Egypt, have you taken us away to die in the wilderness? Why have you so dealt with us, to bring us up out of Egypt? Is this not the word that we told you in Egypt, saying, 'Let us alone that we may serve the Egyptians?' For it would have been better for us to serve the Egyptians than that we should die in the wilderness." And Moses said to the people, "Do not be afraid. Stand still, and see the salvation of the LORD, which He will accomplish for you today. For the Egyptians whom you see today, you shall see again no more forever. The LORD will fight for you, and you shall hold your peace." And the LORD said *to Moses, "Why do you cry to Me? Tell the children of Israel to go forward. But lift up your rod, and stretch out your hand over the sea and divide it. And the children of Israel shall go on dry ground through the midst of the sea.* **Exodus 14:10-16**

To experience a new beginning in your life, it's important for you to look forward and not backwards. In fact, you can't go forward as long as you're looking backwards. The word of the Lord was, tell the children of Israel to go forward.

There are numerous examples in the Word of God where the reader is admonished not to look back. There are dangers in looking back after an ending. Remember Lot's wife. God sent the angel of the Lord to the cities of Sodom and Gomorrah to deliver Lot, his wife, and their two daughters so they would escape the destruction just before God rained down brimstone and fire upon these twin cities. The angel of the Lord came and led Lot and his family out of the city. The angel of the Lord took them forward, not backwards. But the book of Genesis records that Lot's wife looked backed and was turned into a pillar of salt (Genesis 19:24-26). In other words, Lot's wife was indeed leaving those wicked cities, she was moving forward, but she lingered. She lingered in her heart. Her affections were still set on Sodom and Gomorrah. Even though God had delivered her out of this grossly ungodly and wicked place, Sodom and Gomorrah was still in her. She had desire and affection for the luxuries and pleasures of life she enjoyed back in the twin cities. She ascribed much value to the lifestyle there.

When God brings you out of a place, i.e., an ending, you need to understand that place was yesterday. Where you are now is today. Apostle Paul admonished the Philippians with these words:

*Brethren, I do not count myself to have apprehended; but one thing I do, forgetting those things which are behind and reaching forward to those things which are ahead, I press toward the goal for the prize of the upward call of God in Christ Jesus.* Philippians 3:13,14

Paul is clearly saying that he hadn't arrived at his new beginning. The one thing he did, if he didn't do anything else, was to forget those things that were behind him so that he could press forward to those things which lay ahead, i.e., a new beginning. He said that he pressed for the mark, for the prize of the high calling which is in Christ Jesus.

Like Paul, you too are in a race called life,

and there is a finish line. You must press forward toward the mark. Press forward to win the prize of the high calling in Christ Jesus. If you are believing God for a new beginning, that's your high calling, that's your prize. If you are believing God for something significant to change in your life, for an answer to prayer, or for a door to open that has otherwise been closed, if you are believing to come into the fullness of God, your destiny in God, that can be your high calling in God, press on! You want to begin to feel the joy of crossing the finish line and the exhilaration of the tape breaking across your chest. You want to hear the Lord say, *"Well done my good and faithful servant. Enter now into the joy of the Lord!"* (Matthew 25:21,23).

You need to understand something about pressing forward. God wants you to go forward, He wants you to forget about those things that are behind. Why? Because yesterday is your past and the past is dead. Your sins and failures, they're dead. Your defeats and disappointments from yesterday, they're dead. The life you lived in the world, it's dead. The life you lived in the darkness of Egypt is dead. The old life or situation doesn't exist in the mind of God because God is not a God of the dead; He's a God of the living.

God has given us today. We live today and

today is our present. Today is a living reality. God is alive and well today. Today is where you can walk in the nowness of God. Walking in the nowness of God is the very thing that is needful and necessary to move forward. You can't move forward based on history. You can't move forward looking back at death. If you're going to move forward, you must live in the nowness of God, because God is. Isn't that what *Hebrews* said? Hebrews 11:1 says, *"Now faith is ..."* Faith is right now—in the present. If you don't have it right now, you don't have it at all. If you want to talk about what you used to be and the way it used to be, that isn't faith! Faith is now and those that come to God must believe that He is. In other words, God exists now and is a rewarder of those who diligently seek Him. He is a rewarder of those that press forward for the mark, which is the high calling in Christ Jesus. You are living in the nowness of God. Not only is faith now, but the word of God tells us in Revelation 12:10:

*...Now salvation, and strength, and the kingdom of our God, and the power of His Christ have come, for the accuser of our brethren, who accused them before our God day and night, has been cast down.*

Salvation is now. Strength is now. The Kingdom of God is now. The power of Christ is now. The reality of God must always be now because " ... *now is the accepted time; behold, now is the day of salvation* (2 Corinthians 6:2)." Healing, deliverance or whatever blessing or benefit you desire from God is offered to you right now.

Today is your present and tomorrow is your future. If yesterday is your past and today is your present, why is tomorrow your future? Jeremiah 29:11 says:

*For I know the thoughts that I think toward you, says the LORD, thoughts of peace and not of evil, to give you a future and a hope.*

God knows His thoughts toward you. His thoughts are good and not evil, to give you an expected end, i.e., new beginning, to give you a future and a hope. You can have hope for tomorrow, but you will need faith for today. Another way of looking at this when I say yesterday is your past, today is your present, and tomorrow is your future is: yesterday is your mortality, today is your reality, and tomorrow is your destiny. Or I could say, yesterday is your mortality, today is your opportunity, and tomorrow is your destiny. The past is dead, the present is alive, and the future is your hope.

Sometimes life becomes like a treadmill, i.e., you're busy grumbling and complaining— getting all worked up, yet going nowhere. You're just on this thing, and you're not getting anywhere fast. It's just like running in place. You're not going forward, but you're not where you use to be either. Just like the Israelites in (Exodus 14) found themselves in a tough spot, if you will, between a rock and a hard place, have you ever found yourself in a situation where it seemed like there was no way out? Often, when we feel the pressures of life, when we're faced with difficult challenges, our tendency is to murmur and complain, grumble and complain some more. We grumble and complain about everything. We grumble and complain about people, places, and things. If we're not complaining about our spouses, we complain about the children; if we're not complaining about our children, we're complaining about our bosses; if we're not complaining about the boss, then we're complaining about a coworker; if we're not complaining about something at the job, then for sure, we're going to complain about something at church. And more often than not, we're going to complain about the pastor. We're going to complain about someone in visible leadership. If we can't find fault in the pastor or another leader, we always manage to find it in one of the saints in the church.

It's not your brother or your sister—it's you. It's you feeling the tension and conflicts of the discovery zone. It's also you who needs to rise up and go forward and not look back. You must trust God in this "no man's land" and not point the finger and blame other folks.

In this place, God is not a God of comfort. In fact, God will make you uncomfortable. God has a way of stirring up the nest so that we can mount up with wings as eagles and begin to fly (Isaiah 40:31). It's time to go forward, to spread your wings and fly. Your situation won't change until you change in your resolve to go forward. The same situation you faced yesterday, you ought not be facing today, because God is a living reality, and He is here and He has sent his word to heal us and to deliver us from all of our destruction (Psalm 107:20). The power of the Lord is still present today to heal and help in this uncomfortable place. You can't have a new beginning without going forward.

Often, the impediment to going forward comes down to whether we react or respond in the face of challenge and crisis. Instead of responding with faith and thanksgiving when we find ourselves facing a test or trial, we find ourselves reacting with doubt, fear, unbelief, wanting, and despair.

Israel failed to respond with faith and thanksgiving. When they found themselves closed in by Pharaoh's mighty army in hot pursuit from the rear, and the Red Sea, vast and deep in front of them, instead of being mindful that

God was the One who had already worked great signs, wonders, and miracles, they forgot. They were unmindful that God wrought a mighty deliverance for them to bring them as far as they had gone. They didn't focus on the goodness and greatness of God. They didn't focus on the now God who rules today. Instead, they focused on their doubts, fears, the Red Sea, and Pharaoh's mighty army. In other words, they reacted.

God doesn't want us to be reactionary. To react is something that doesn't take any faith. It doesn't take any confidence to react. To react simply means that you are acting in return to opposition, to crisis, to challenge, a test or trial. It's an emotional reflex, a knee-jerk reaction. Have you ever gone to a physician for a complete physical? The physician will ask you to sit on the edge of the table. He'll take this little rubber hammer and he'll tap you on the knee. As soon as the hammer makes contact with the knee, you involuntarily kick your leg out in reaction. That is why it is called a knee-jerk reaction. A lot of people have given nothing more than a knee jerk reaction to the crises, challenges, tests or trials in their lives. You may be going through a difficult place on your journey. Perhaps you've given nothing more than a knee-jerk reaction. God doesn't want you to react. He wants you to respond. He wants you to respond with faith and thanksgiving (1 Thessalonians 5:18).

There is definitely a difference between re-acting and responding. When we react, we're doing nothing more than acting in return to some situation. That's all we're doing. How-ever, when we respond, we're answering the situation with ability and with purpose. We're answering the situation with the ability of God and the destiny of God in mind. Our attitude is: "I ain't going to let nobody turn me around. I'm not going to let nobody cause me to turn back. God brought me this far to take me on to something better." Now if you look at the word "respond," it's the verb form of the noun "re-sponsibility." The word "responsibility" is re-ally two words in one: response ability. It means the ability to respond. In God you have the ability to respond. You have the ability to respond to Pharaoh and his army. You have the ability to respond to the Red Sea that stands before you. It doesn't matter how mas-sive your mountain may be, how tall your giant may be, you have the ability in God to respond. The response God is looking for is a response in faith. He's looking for a response in thanks-giving—an attitude of gratitude. Why? Be-cause you can praise Him and thank Him today because of the great miracles He did yesterday. He delivered you out of the muck and the mire; He delivered you out of the darkness of Egypt; He brought you out of, an impossible situation. That same God who delivered you with an outstretched arm and a mighty hand, is the same God who can deliver you today from Pharaoh's army and the Red Sea.

We need to remember the goodness of God. We need to forget the things in the past, but remember the God of the past who delivered us from our darkness and brought us to the light of this present time (1 Peter 2:9). We need to remember that. If you're not careful, you'll find yourself focusing on yesterday. You'll find yourself focusing on that which is dead, that which is lifeless, that which has no power, that which has no energy. Yesterday is like a television rerun. Reruns can be very boring to watch. This is the day that the Lord hath made, rejoice and be glad in it (Psalm 118:24). God did not bring you this far to leave you now!

## CHAPTER ELEVEN

# What Do You Do When You Feel Trapped?

*And Moses said to the people, "Do not be afraid. Stand still, and see the salvation of the LORD, which He will accomplish for you today. For the Egyptians whom you see today, you shall see again no more forever. The LORD will fight for you, and you shall hold your peace.*
**Exodus 14:13,14**

Many have felt trapped just like the Israelites did. What do you do when you feel trapped? What do you do when you find yourself in a situation, in a relationship, on a job that's a dead-end, going nowhere? You can't turn to the right, you can't turn to the left, you can't go forward, it seems, because the Red Sea is in front of you, and you can't go backwards because the enemy is in hot pursuit of you and seeks to destroy you. So what do you do when you feel trapped on a dead-end street?

When you are closed in on every side, when you can't do anything else, just look up! God will always give you the grace to look up. Yes, you can look up, as the Word says, I will lift up my eyes unto the hills from whence comes my help, for it comes from the Lord (Psalm 121:1). In Exodus 14 verse 13, Moses said unto the people, " ...Do not be afraid." Fear is the enemy of faith. Fear is the problem in every situation. Fear will attack at its own time. There are a lot of bad things that can happen in your life because of your fears. If you operate in fear, you will attract bad and negative circumstances. Remember what Job went through. Job lost his wealth, his children. He lost everything he had and Job said, "the thing I greatly fear is come upon me (Job 3:25)." What am I saying? According to Job, the things you're going through, the hard places you've fallen upon, these are the very things you may have been afraid of.

My wife was sharing with me on the way to the church one Sunday morning that this internationally-known female singer was in a really bad accident. A semi-tractor truck rammed into the rear end of her tour bus. The singer sustained a broken back and was threatened with paralysis. But God gave her a miracle. God healed her spinal cord. God not only restored her health to where she's touring and singing again, but she's still dancing like she did in the early days of her professional career. Thank

God that she gives Him all the glory for this miracle.

What was interesting about this story, as my wife and I conversed, is that while growing up, this singer's father was confined in a wheelchair. He eventually withered and died in the wheelchair. Throughout this singer's life, she lived in fear. She had a fear that she was going to end up like her father, that her plight in life would be like her father's. I believe that, because of this fear, these bad circumstances came upon her. But thank God, He gave her crop failure. She didn't permanently reap the seed of fear she had sown for much of her life. God turned her captivity as He did Job's (Job 42:10).

Fear will cause you to be defeated before the enemy will ever defeat you. When you feel trapped and closed in, when there's no way out, as Moses said to the children of Israel,

"...stand still ..." (v.13). Just stand still. If you'll stand still, lift up your eyes and look unto the hills from whence comes your help, you'll find that the battle is not yours— it's God's. This battle that you've been fighting is not your battle, it's the Lord's. Moses further said to Israel, stand still and see the deliverance of the Lord, which he shall accomplish for you today. God is a Deliverer of today. God is a right-now God. If you stand still, God will bring about a powerful deliverance; and he will do it today.

The "Egyptians" that are coming after you to destroy you, God says you will not see them again any more forever (v.13). If you'll trust God when you feel trapped and begin to give God thanksgiving and your faith, you'll find that, in your problem, your crisis, your challenge, God will give you victory over it. Some people are still repeating the lessons of yesterday, the lessons of three, five, ten years ago. Why? They refused to stand still. They refused to be thankful and have faith in God. Often we talk ourselves into greater trouble. We dig an even greater pit, an even deeper ditch.

We need to learn to trust God. If God saved us, if God brought us from what we used to be and where we used to be, then, won't that same God deliver us now? Won't that same God come to your rescue? You've got to stand still and know that He's God. You will see His deliverance in your life today. You don't have to worry about the giants. You don't have to worry about the Pharaohs. You don't have to worry about whatever is bothering you and plaguing you, even if a great army is chasing you. You can know beyond a shadow of a doubt that the same God of yesterday is God today and will be God forever (Hebrews 13:8).

*The Lord will fight for you, and you shall*

*hold your peace* (Verse 14). This may seem crude, but we must learn to shut up and wait on God. Can you imagine this scenario: the Israelites are in a panic. They have made their journey from Succoth to Etham. They're at the edge of the wilderness. They have been set free and liberated as slaves. They've gone this far on a promise, driven by a vision of destiny that God will lead them into a land that flows with milk and honey. All of a sudden, they lose their excitement about God. Suddenly, they stop singing the song of the Lord and their thoughts shift to thinking that it would have been better had they stayed in Egypt. They begin to accuse Moses of bringing them into the wilderness to die. They raised the question: "Weren't there enough graves in Egypt?" Sure, there were enough graves in Egypt, but these people had a hostile sarcasm towards Moses. Egypt was known for it's elaborate pyramids and its tombs. They may have made these accusations sar- castically, but their hostility was unmistakeable.

Like some people, they just want to walk up to the leader and tell him/her off. They want to cuss him/her out. They'll use their sarcasm to express suppressed hostility toward the leader and vent what they believe the leader ought to be doing—their way rather than God's way. Sometimes when people are faced with the Red Sea and feel the pressures of Pharaoh's army coming behind them, they panic. They panic and feel the need to point the finger at someone else again, usually the leader. They need somebody to blame; somebody to make them feel good about their plight. So they begin to scream and cry out to God because they can't get across the Red Sea. It is too deep and too wide, and they cannot go backwards because Pharaoh's army is turning up the heat. All they see is Pharaoh's army and the Red Sea. They lose faith to see that the God who created them is the same God who made the Red Sea and created Pharaoh. They don't have the vision to see the greatness of God; they only have faith to see their problems.

We can be good at identifying the problem, talking about the problem, but we're very poor at appropriating the answer. The God we serve is the answer to every question, the solution to every problem, and the supplier to every need (Philippians 4:19).

### A Time to Pray and A Time to Obey

*And the LORD said to Moses, "Why do you cry to Me? Tell the children of Israel to go forward* (Exodus 14:15). The children of Israel cried to Moses rather than to God. Moses was a good leader. Moses had a soft heart, and he began to pray to God on behalf of the people. Moses loved these people so much that he got himself out of the will of God. In fact God, on

102

one occasion, sought to destroy these uncir-
cumcised, stiff-necked people. Moses stood
between God and the people, and as a result,
Moses was precluded from going into the Promised Land. God gave him a view of the land, but
did not allow his feet to touch the land.
(Deuteronomy 34:1-5).

When Israel began to accuse Moses and cry
out in fear, Moses, being the gracious leader he
was, began to pray to God. Isn't it interesting
what God says in His answer to Moses' prayer?
God said to Moses, "why are you praying to
Me?" Now this is enough to mess up your
theology on prayer. A lot of us think we need to
pray, pray, pray, and pray. God said to Moses,
why are you praying to me? Tell the children of
Israel to go forward. Often times we find ourselves praying about something over and over
and over again, only to postpone what God has
already told us to do. There's a time to pray and
there's a time to obey. You cannot use prayer
as a substitute for disobedience or for obedience. When God has given you a directive, you
don't pray about it, you begin to walk in it.
When God gives you direction, if you'll begin to
step out in what He's given you, He'll guide you
step by step. You can pray all you want, and
you'll find yourself stuck right where you are in
the discovery zone.

Moses prayed and God answered. God said,

"why are you praying to Me?" He said tell the children of Israel to go forward (verse 15). In other words, tell the people that the vision has not changed. Tell them that the authority of the vision is the same.

When you know what you ought to be doing, when you know what God has said to you, when you know what the Word of God says, why do you have to pray about what the Word has told you to do? For example, if the Bible tells you to walk in love, don't pray about loving someone. You had better find yourself loving them if you're going to be in the will of God. You can pray all you want and still have an unloving heart. The word says we're to walk in love (Ephesians 5:2). You don't pray about loving somebody, you just love him or her.

Some people pray about paying a tithe to the Lord. You don't pray about paying your tithes; he already told you to do that (Malachi 3:8-12). There's a time to pray and a time to obey. If the Word says bring ye all the tithes to the storehouse, you don't pray about that; you do that. You can no longer hide behind prayer as an excuse for doing nothing and for being nothing in God.

Many who pray don't truly understand prayer. Moses did. Prayer is simply talking to God, and we talk to God from our hearts. We don't need a flowery religious speech to approach our Heavenly Father. We don't need to wax theologically eloquent. The same way my kids talk to me and make their request of me is the way we ought to come before the throne of grace, with boldness, to obtain mercy and to find help in our time of need (Hebrews 4:16). We talk to God the same way we talk to each other. Don't talk to God like he's some inanimate object. Don't talk to God like he's somewhere in outer space. God lives in you. You can talk to him any time you want to.

Some people say that prayer changes things. Think about it. Does prayer really change things? On one level, it certainly seems that way. But on a higher level, prayer really doesn't change things. Prayer changes people, and people change things. God will use people to change things, as a result of prayer (Philippians 2:13). Some people think that when they pray things happen. Well, they might as well come off that ego trip. Things do not happen when we talk to God, things happen when God talks to us! So when you pray, hear what God says to you. If you've been down on your knees running your mouth for an hour and you haven't allowed God to say anything, I would consider you very rude person. Things did not happen when Moses prayed to God, but things happened when God spoke to Moses (Exodus 14:15-23). If you are praying, and you're not hearing from God, it's time to shut up and listen. Let God get a word in edgewise...side ways ... some kind of way.

God said to Moses, why are you praying to me? Tell the children of Israel to go forward. God was saying to Moses, Moses I've already given you the vision. Moses, I've already given you direction. Moses, I've already given you my Word, I've already told you that you are to tell Pharaoh to let my people go that they may worship me in the wilderness, that you may bring my people into Canaan Land, a land flowing with milk and honey. God essentially said, my vision is the same, the instructions are the same, so why are you praying to me?

### A Vision and Its Authority

*But lift up your rod, and stretch out your hand over the sea and divide it. And the children of Israel shall go on dry ground through the midst of the sea* (Exodus 14:16). God is here saying: Moses, I've given you the vision and the authority to support the vision. Every vision needs an authority. When God spoke to Moses in Exodus Chapter 3 from of the burning bush, God gave Moses the vision then and there. He gave Moses His plan and purpose and destiny for Israel. God told Moses to pick up the rod and put it in his hand. "By this rod I will work signs, wonders, and miracles." The rod became the authority for the vision.

When Moses met with Pharaoh, and when Pharaoh resisted Moses, Moses would take the rod of God, and God would work a miracle. Again, this rod speaks of authority and there is an authority with every vision. If you have a vision for your life, if you have a vision for your family, if you have a vision for your job, if you have a vision for your ministry, then what is the authority for that vision? The authority is the rod; the authority is the Word of God. Your vision must be supported by the Word of God— no exceptions. It has to be undergirded with the Word of God. If your vision doesn't match the Word of God, it is not a God-given vision. *For whatsoever is born of God overcometh the world: and this is the victory that overcometh the world, even our faith* (1 John 5:4).

When God puts the rod in your hand, no one else is to take it out of your hand. A leader can't go any further until the people go forward. God didn't say to Moses, "Moses go forward." He said, Moses, tell the children of Israel to go forward. In the context of the local church, the pastor can't go any further until the people go forward. As long as the people are stuck on yesterday, as long as the people are tied to the past, the pastor must keep preaching and teaching messages to free them. When your vehicle is stuck in the mud, you can spin your wheels all you want, you can murmur and complain about being late for an appointment, but as long as that wheel is spinning in the mud—you're stuck in the mud— you're still where you are. You can't move forward until you get out of the mud. God said, "tell the people to go forward."

You can not lead people where they don't want to go. If you're in a relationship with somebody, whether it's a spouse, boyfriend or girlfriend, you can't lead them where they don't want to go. Often times our lives are punctuated by conflict, stress, and tension because we're trying to drag people to where we think they ought to go. You can only lead people to where they want to go. Moses could not lead Israel to Canaan Land if they didn't want to go.

Remember when Israel left Egypt, instead of heading to Canaan Land, they camped at the edge of the wilderness. Perhaps they found some comfort there. However, it took the threats of Pharaoh's army to motivate them to go on from there. Moses could never have led them to a place they didn't want to go to. So God told Moses to tell the people to go forward.

There was a young lady in the first church I pastored. She was a very talented young person. She was a homeowner, drove a luxury car, had money and a good career; in fact, she held a very significant position within city government. She had all this going on, but she was single, never married. She had waited many years for God to send "Mr. Right" along. She had everything going for her, and she sure didn't need a "zero." All of a sudden, she met this guy and telephoned me and said, "Oh, Pastor Jerry, I'm so happy. I have met "Mr. Right." This guy and I get along, we do things together, we enjoy each other's company, on and on and on." Some months later, while on a ministry visit to her city, I asked her how things were going between her and this guy. She answered, "Well Pastor Jerry, I had to drop him. I asked what happened. She said, "Pastor Jerry, I'm single, I've never been married, and I always had a vision of having children. This guy had been previously married, and he had some children, and he doesn't want any more children. We did not share the same vision." So she had to drop him. You can't lead people to where they don't want to go. Why waste your time with a man who doesn't want to have children if your desire and vision is for child-bearing. Don't waste your time. Don't tell me you're going to change him. You can't change him. You must rise up and go forward. Either he's going to come along, or you'll meet some-body else along the way.

If you want to go forward, but you can't find a way to go forward, and you still find yourself stuck on yesterday, it's because: you don't have a vision or you don't believe in the vision you say you have. If you have a vision, that vision will energize you. That vision will fuel you and cause you to be thrust from where you are to where God wants you to be, into a new beginning. In other words, we live and we die with what we believe. We live and we die by our vision. If you can't rise up and go forward, if you keep finding yourself looking backwards, then you really have to ask yourself if you really have a vision. If you don't have a vision, you need to come and get in the presence of God and be still and know that he's God, hold your peace and let God birth a vision in your heart.

It bears repeating: you can't lead people where they don't want to go. Can two walk together except they be agreed? (Amos 3:3). Everybody has to be singing from the same sheet of music and be on the same page. This is the problem in many marriages. This is the problem in the workplace. People aren't on the same page. The way you get people on the same page is not by trying to change them. You rise up and go forward. Tell them to go forward. God didn't say, Moses you go forward and they're going to follow you. No, he said, tell them to go forward. If you don't like what's happening in your marriage or on your job, stop trying to change things with strong-arm tactics. You simply need to rise up and go forward. You do what's right. You obey the

Word of God. You walk in the will of God. Your spouse, boss, and coworkers will catch up with you.

## Walking the Talk in the Discovery Zone

In Genesis Chapter 11, at the tower of Babel, the inhabitants of the earth came together in the plain of Shinar and said, let us build a tower who's top reaches into the heavens. God came down, the Bible says, to the city and looked at the tower. God said "For the people are of one language and the people are of one mind and one purpose." He said, "Let us go down among them and confuse their language that they might be scattered abroad." God didn't want a tower to be built unto heaven. God didn't want a tower built for the purposes of idolatry and star gazing. For He was the true God and only God. So God said, we've got to do something about this, we've got to confuse their language, because these people are all speaking a common language. These people are of one mind and one purpose. In other words, when people get together and are on the same page, speaking one language, being of one mind and purpose, there is nothing impossible unto that people. This is also resounded in I Corinthians 1:10: *Now I plead with you, brethren, by the name of our Lord Jesus Christ, that you all speak the same thing, and that there be no divisions among you, but that you be perfectly joined together in the same mind and in the same judgment.*

Paul says, I want you to speak the same thing. He says, I don't want there to be any divisions among you. One of the greatest manifestations of unity is when those you are joined with begin to say the same thing. When you can say the same thing, then you can be the same. Let there be no divisions among you, but let us be of the same judgment, of the same mind, in one accord with one another. In others words, you can't lead people where they don't want to go. You just can't talk the talk. If you're going to rise up and go forward and refuse to look back, you can't just talk about it. You've got to walk the walk. To walk the walk means that you have to embody this thing through mental assimilation, heart-felt integration, and with bold articulation. Such assimilation, coupled with visceral integration and articulation, will always produce the manifestation of walking what you talk (2 Corinthians 4:13).

## CHAPTER TWELVE

# Rise Up and Go Forward

---

*Then I said to them, "You see the distress that we are in, how Jerusalem lies waste, and its gates are burned with fire. Come and let us build the wall of Jerusalem, that we may no longer be a reproach." And I told them of the hand of my God which had been good upon me, and also of the king's words that he had spoken to me. So they said, "Let us rise up and build." Then they set their hands to this good work.* **(Nehemiah 2:17,18)**

If I may borrow from William Bridges, author of *Managing Transitions*, there are four things you need to embody if you are going to rise up, go forward and launch a new beginning:

- Purpose
- Picture
- Plan
- Part to Play

The first thing you need is purpose. You must have some kind of outcome in mind that you seek. You must have a sense of vision, a sense of destiny. What is your purpose for wanting to go forward? The idea behind Israel's journey through the wilderness was that they had been oppressed in Egypt. A new beginning in a land of their own, as promised by God, was certainly something they could understand. It was a solution to their problems in Egypt. It answered the question, "Why are we going forward?" A major obstacle to a new beginning is that there is no discernable purpose behind the anticipated and desired change.

Second, after purpose, you need a picture. Although purpose is critical to new beginnings, they can be rather abstract. They are ideas, and most people need more than an idea to commit to a risky undertaking. They need something they can see, or at least imagine. A picture is experiencing the outcome; in other words, you want to experience your destiny. You want to experience your new beginning first and foremost through your imagination. If you can conceive it in your mind, you can believe it in your heart. If you can't mentally conceive it in your mind, you have no imagination. For example, if you're sick and you can't even imagine how it would feel if you were healed, then what makes you think you will ever be healed? If your marriage is on the rocks and you can't imagine how it would be if you had marital bliss and happiness, then how can you reasonably expect God to heal your marriage? If you're unemployed and you can't imagine how it would be to have a job and pay your own bills, how can you reasonably expect to move forward and get a job?

After you have purpose and a picture, then you need a plan. The creation of a plan is the result of responding to the picture in your mind in a way that captures your imagination. You need a clear idea of how you are going to get from where you are to where you believe God wants you to be. You must be open to God making adjustments to your plan. God will give us direction, but we don't get His guidance until we start moving. You have to have a plan to get from where you are to where you want to be.

The last thing you need is a part to play. No one is going to do it for you. If you're going to experience a new beginning, you must rise up and go forward. The word of the Lord to Moses was to tell the people to go forward. He didn't say go find some folks to carry these folks over. Nobody is going to do it for you. You must do it for yourself. You have to have a part to play. You must clearly see your role and your responsibility in the overall scheme of things. In other words, you have to be willing to contribute and participate in a tangible way to getting from the edge of the wilderness to your new beginning.

What are you willing to give? What are you willing to sacrifice? What are you willing to do? This is not a time to look at yesterday. Yesterday is dead. As in the words of Nehemiah, who had a strong sense of purpose to return to Jerusalem, rebuild the walls of the city and restore temple worship, driven by a clear vision (picture) and Divinely inspired plan, he urged the people of Israel, in the face of opposition, to "… rise up and build." Those Israelites who wanted change in their city had a part to play; they had to contribute and participate in a tangible way. They had to be the ones who worked on rebuilding the walls of Jerusalem; they had to be the ones who would be willing to fight the enemies of God who posed a threat to their enjoying a new beginning in the rebuilding of Jerusalem.

God has given you this day. Today is your day of opportunity, and God will never take you anywhere that His grace won't keep you. So rise up, go forward and don't look back!

# Conclusion

---

*There can be no more important task than understanding and mastering change.*

**~George Land and Beth Jarman**

*Unless transition occurs, change will not work.*

**~William Bridges**

*Every beginning is a consequence. Every beginning ends something.*

**~Agnes Allen**

None of our lives are exempt from change. Change is something everyone has to deal with, whether you want to or not. But unless you understand change and transition, the process will not work. After a change occurs, a transition begins. Change is significantly different from transition. Change is external and situational. Transition is internal and emotional. Every change means something has ended and something starts with a new beginning. There is an internal transition process between endings and new beginnings.

There are three phases to change and transition: endings, exploration, and new beginnings. The implications of these processes are: when something ends, a typical reaction can be a sense of loss, a feeling of grief, and a struggle to let go of the past. Every ending gives birth to an exploration (transition). Explorations are emblematic of what Israel experienced in their wilderness journeying. As in the case of the nation Israel, you too will go through a discovery zone, being in a temporary state between the old and the new, the past and the future. In this phase of the process, you will perceive the change with a sense of loss or gain. It is here where you discover suppressed thoughts and feelings you have about God, others, and yourselves. In this deeply emotional zone, depending on how you react, this can be an opportunity for chaos or creativity. After the change and transition occur, the new beginning, although a new opportunity, can present feelings that energize you, as well as make you feel awkward and uncertain. In other words, in the new beginning you will feel a little shaky but excited at the same time.

The way of the wilderness is a discovery zone that depicts, metaphorically, the phases of change and transition that both individuals and organizations undergo. A changed situation can be brought about suddenly; however, a transition into a new beginning takes time not for the sake of time, but for the purposes of discovery and learning. As with Israel, God won't usher you into a promised new beginning until you have learned all the lessons of your wilderness. Not that God is slow in delivering His promises, rather, the people of God are often slow in learning needed spiritual lessons.

The way of the wilderness starts with an ending and finishes with a new beginning. The prolonged tests and trials and hardships of working your way through a transition should always be viewed as a time of proving and preparation for the anticipated new beginning. No one in his or her right mind wants to take forty years to make a several-day transition, as Israel did. The temptation of shortcutting the process is appealing, but deceiving. It will prolong and possibly abort the new beginning. The longest time and distance between two points, in terms of an emotionally-led transition, is a shortcut. It takes a process of time to get in touch with your thoughts and feelings and to let go of something. Furthermore, it takes even more mental preparation to accept what comes after letting go. Moreover, in this state of limbo between the old and the new, it is extremely difficult to quickly resolve this identity crisis.

Although the new beginning is ready for you, you may not be ready for it. However, you must be committed to learning the lessons of the wilderness (transition) in order to move on. You can't go forward as long as you are holding on to the past; neither can you enjoy a new beginning if you feel trapped in an uncertain place in the wilderness. In the words of the Lord given to Moses, "tell the [people] to go forward." Moving on is your great challenge. Going forward in the change and transition process requires a commitment to the author- ity of your God-given vision, obedience to the Word of God, and an eager willingness to change.

It is imperative to patiently work through change and transition and resist the tempta- tion to prematurely escape this "uncomfort" zone. Unless a successful transition occurs, change will not work! After something ends, if change doesn't occur, then you are stuck between nowhere and somewhere. Again, you need to view this time as an opportunity for self-discovery, and to learn about your attitudes towards others and rediscover the faith-fulness of God. Notwithstanding the harsh conditions of your desert, God's presence is always with you, no matter how unbearable things seems. God, for the sake of His glory, has a vested interest in leading and guiding you to your new beginning. In the Discovery Zone, your steps are ordered by the Lord!

You may contact the author by the
following address:

**Dr. Jerry M. Williams**
c/o Vision Books
4625 North Keystone Avenue
Indianapolis, Indiana 46205

*(317) 257-2687*
*JerryWilliams@visionbooks.com*